Learn To Draw Pokemon - 10 Simple Characters: Pencil Drawing Step By Step Book 2

Pencil Drawing Ideas for Absolute Beginners

By Jeet Gala

Published By:

Gala Publication

ISBN-13: 978-1512108576
ISBN-10: 151210857X

©Copyright 2015 – Gala Publication

Table of Contents

Aron

Step 1

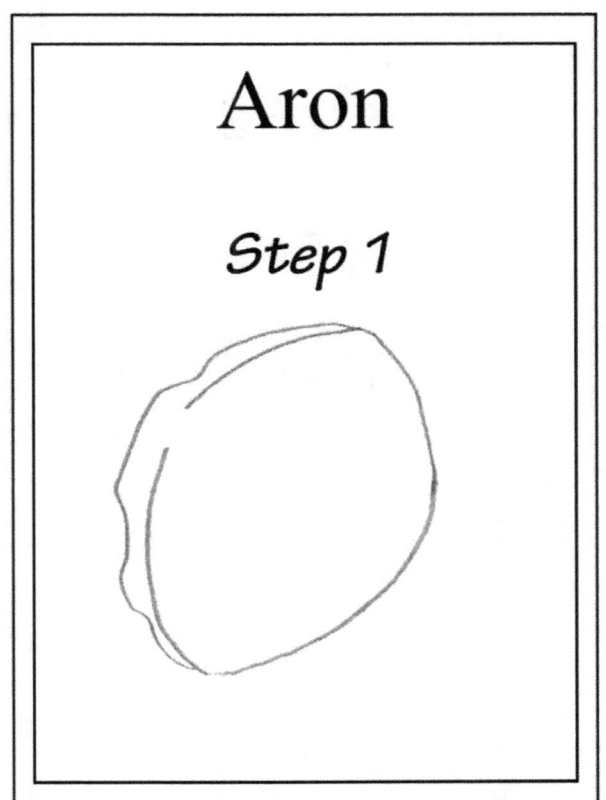

Step 2

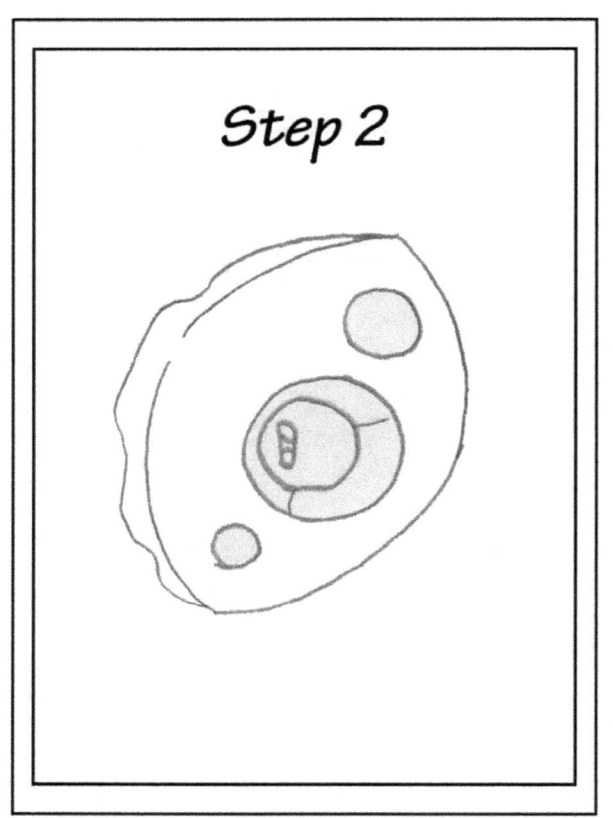

Step 3

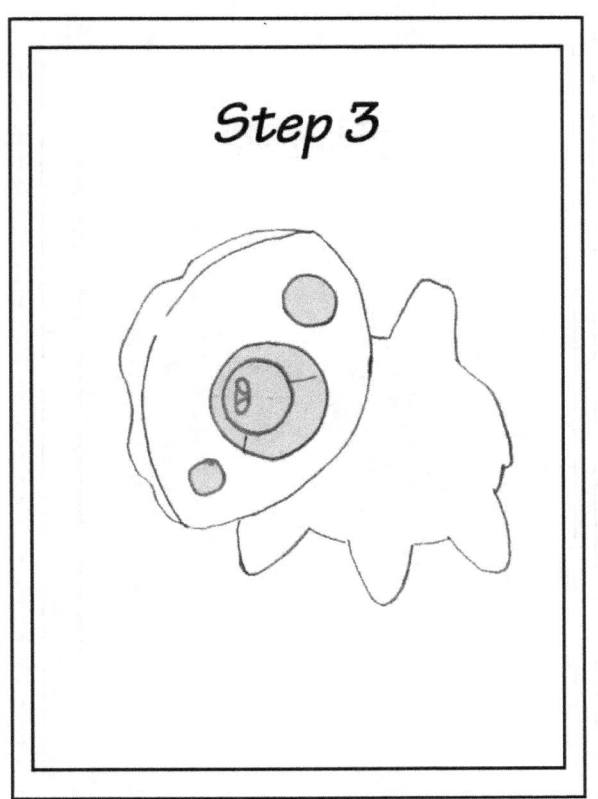

Step 4

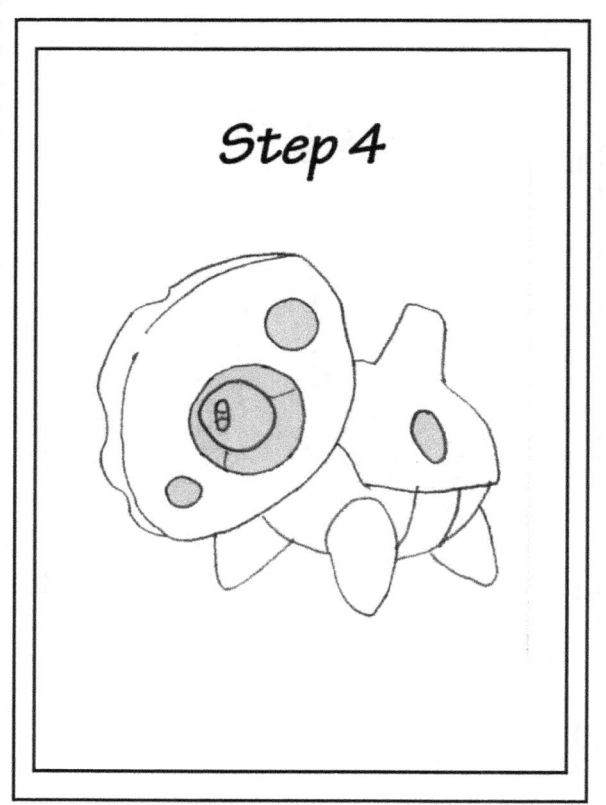

Marill

Step 1

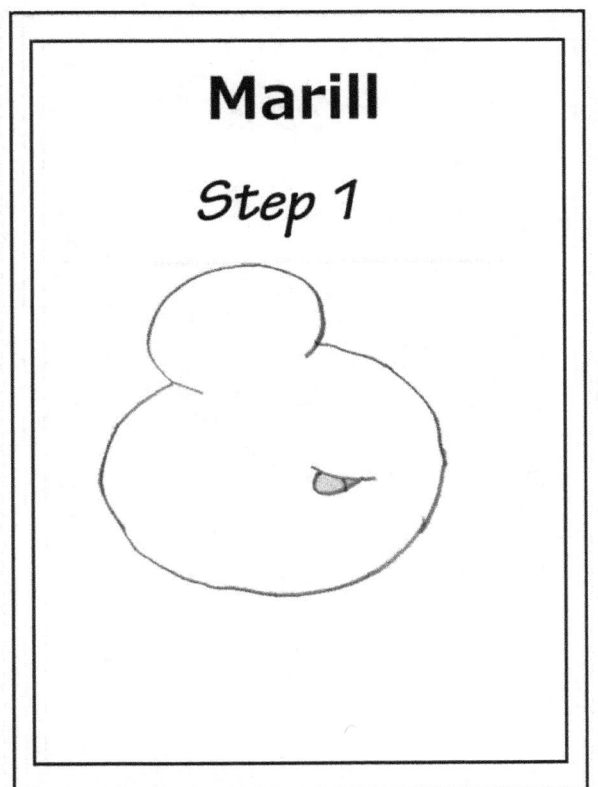

Step 2

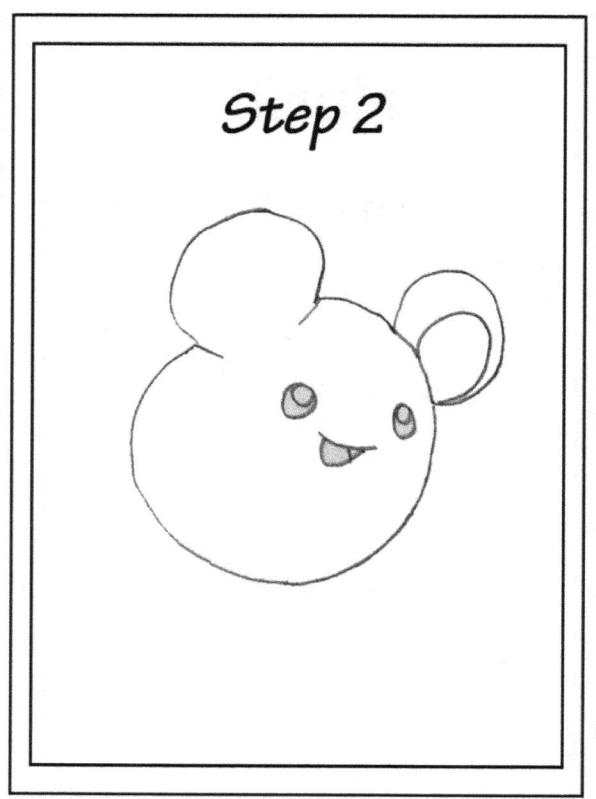

Step 3

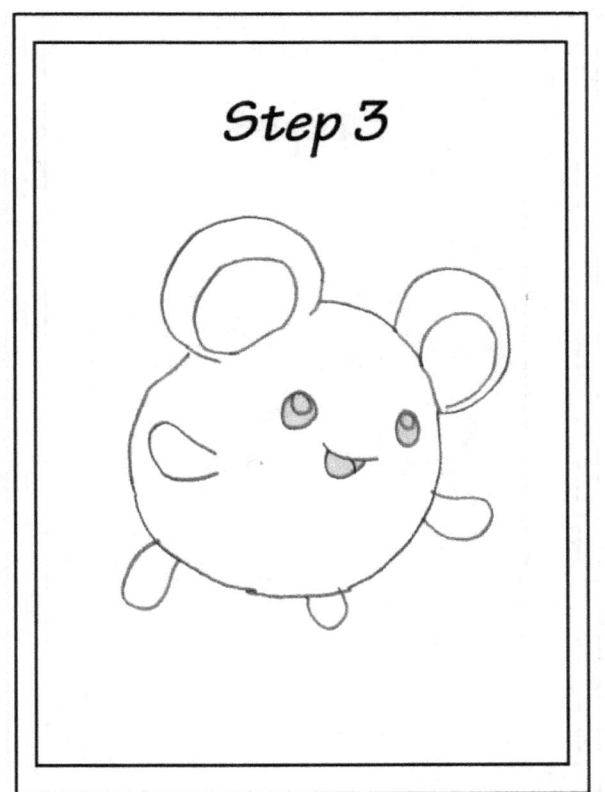

Step 4

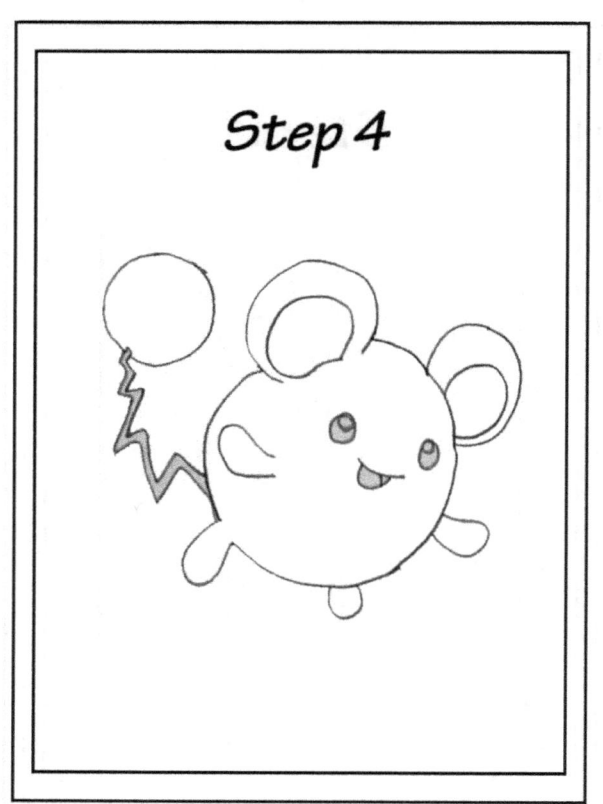

Froakie

Step 1

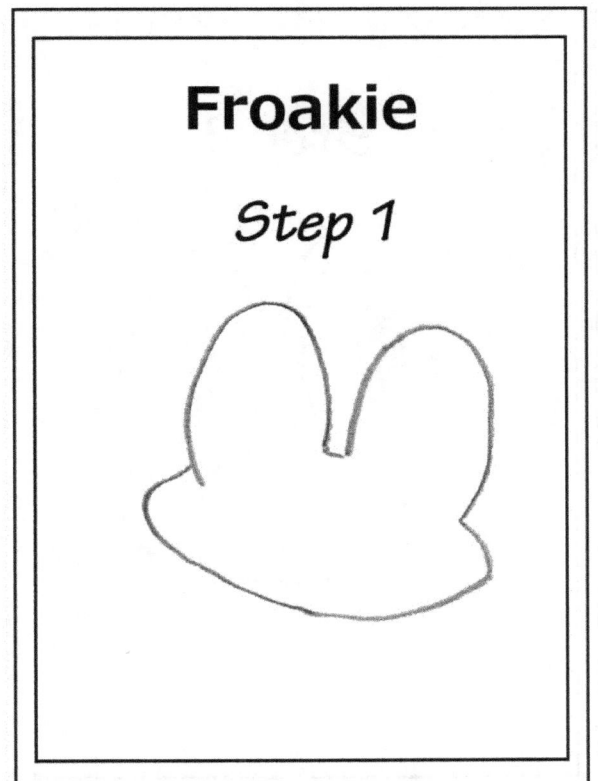

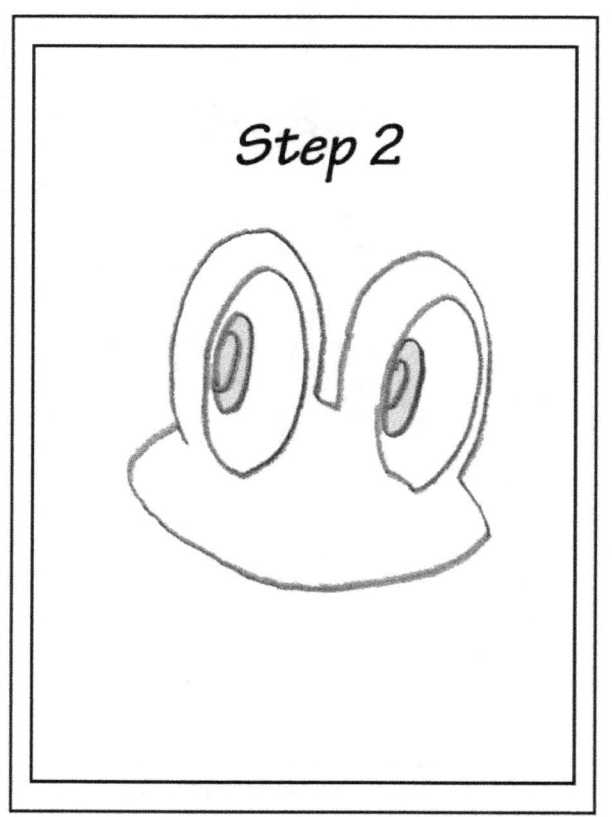

Step 2

Step 3

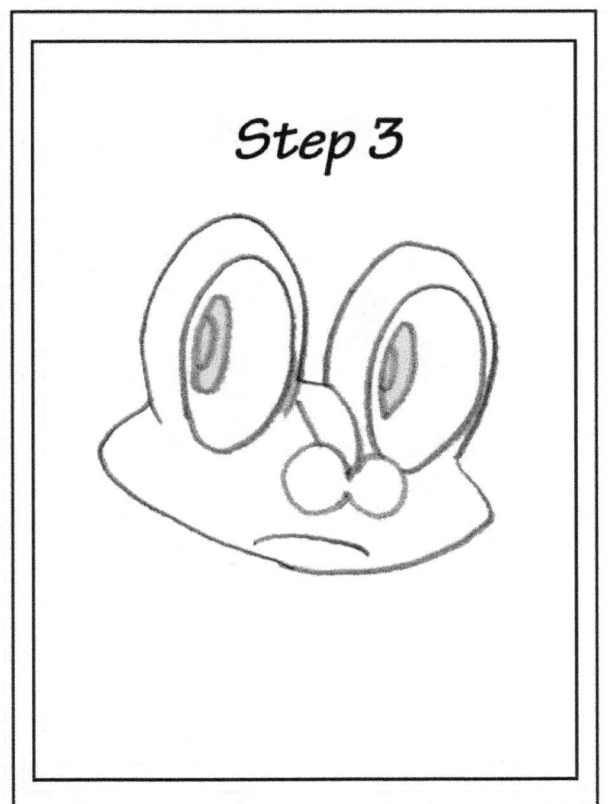

Step 4

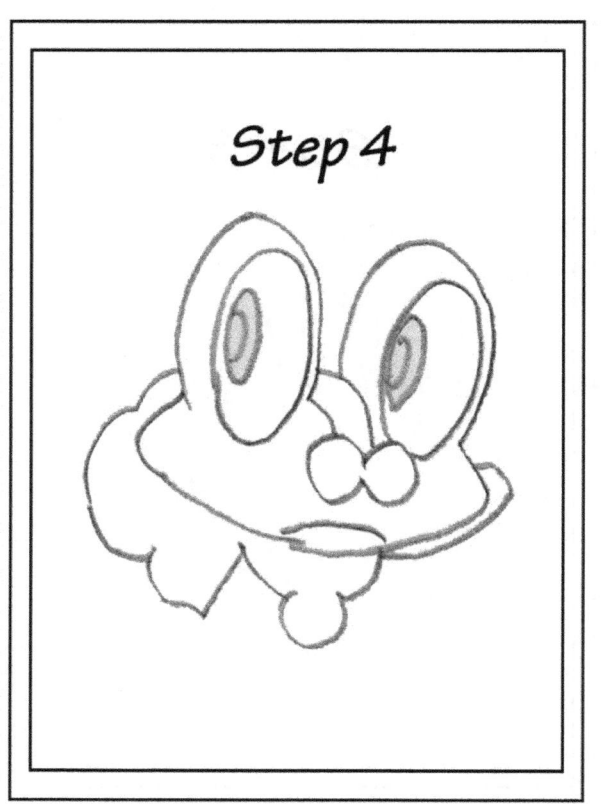

Step 5

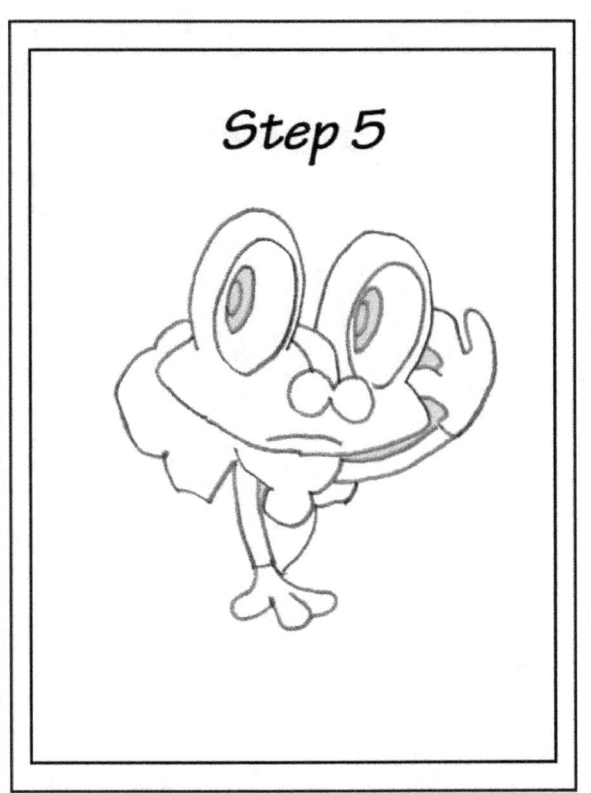

Step 6

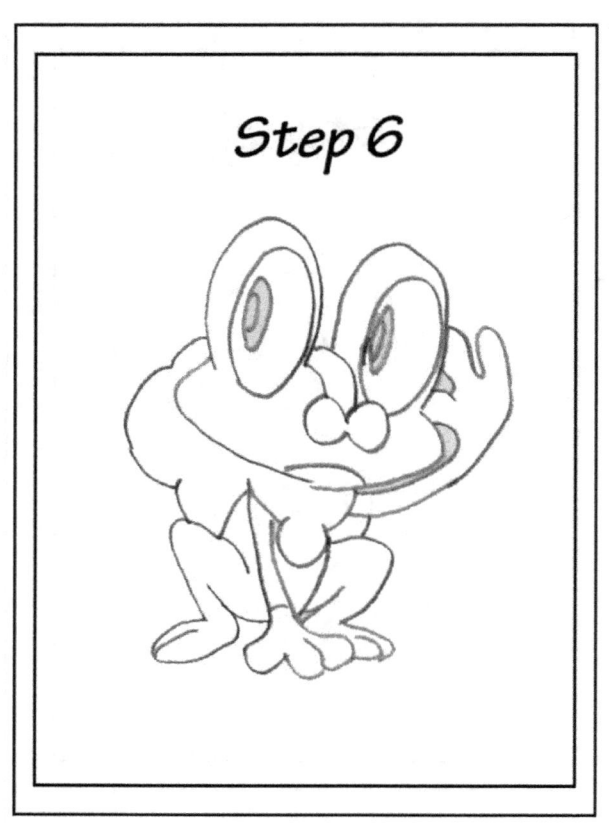

Beautifly

Step 1

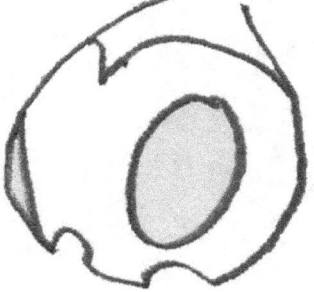

Step 2

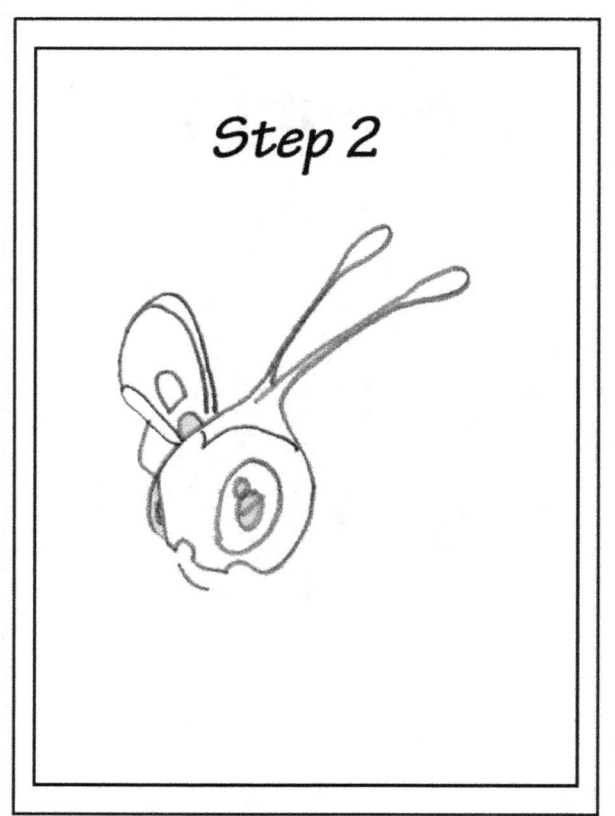

Step 3

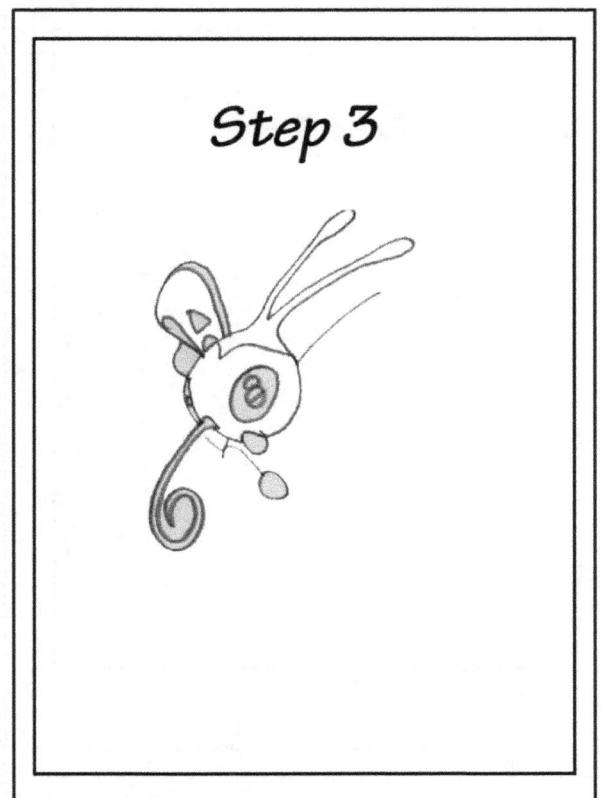

Step 4

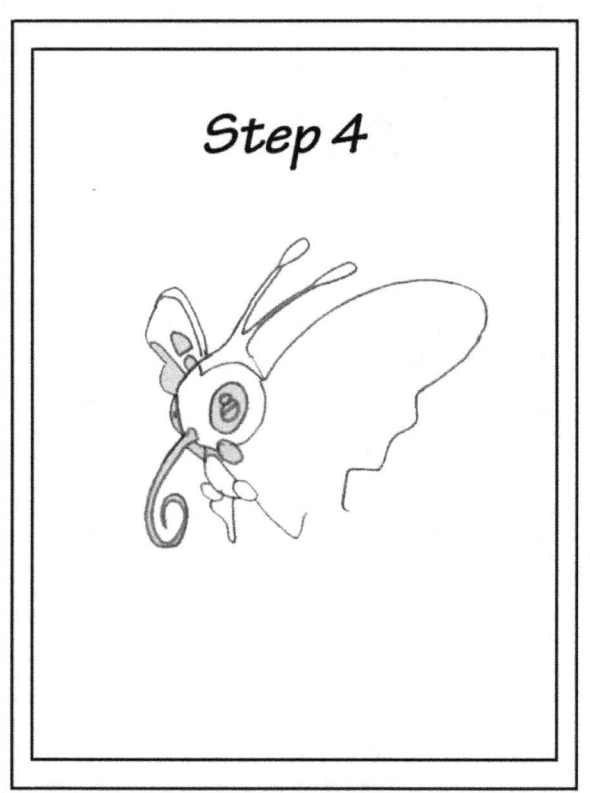

Step 5

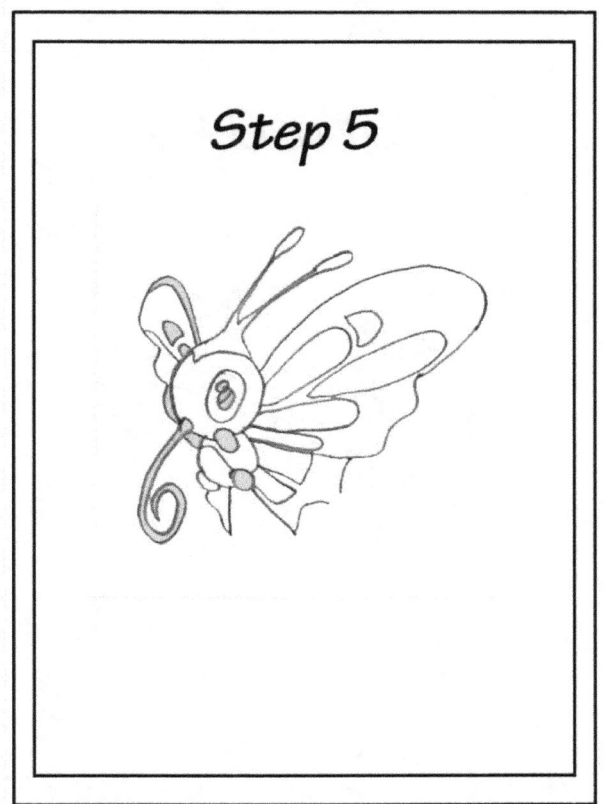

Step 6

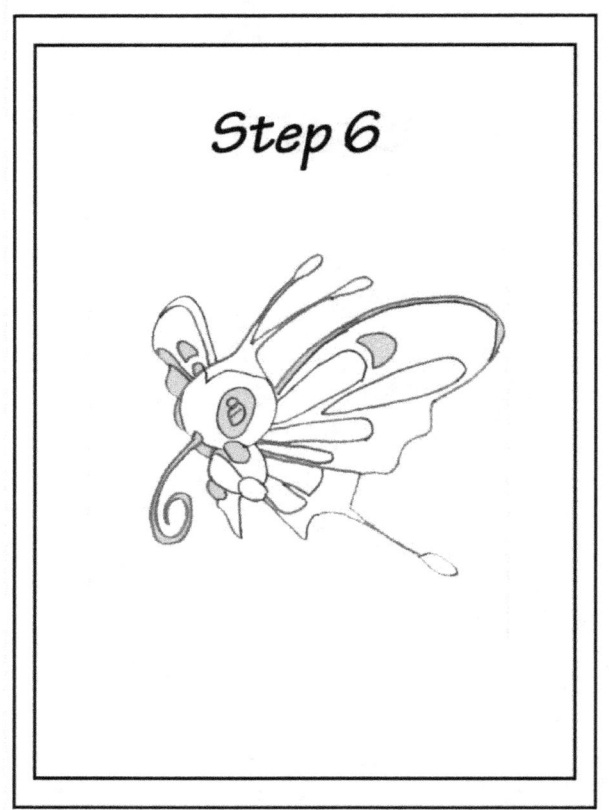

Celebi

Step 1

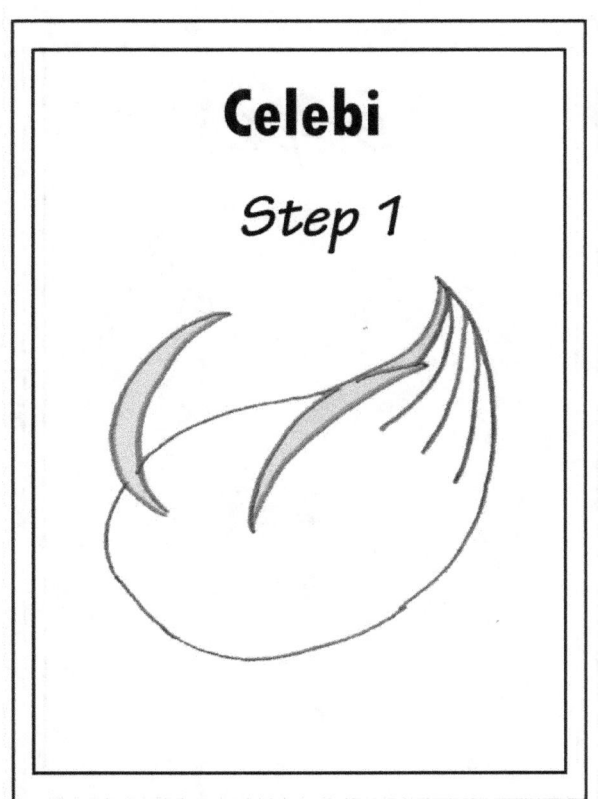

Step 2

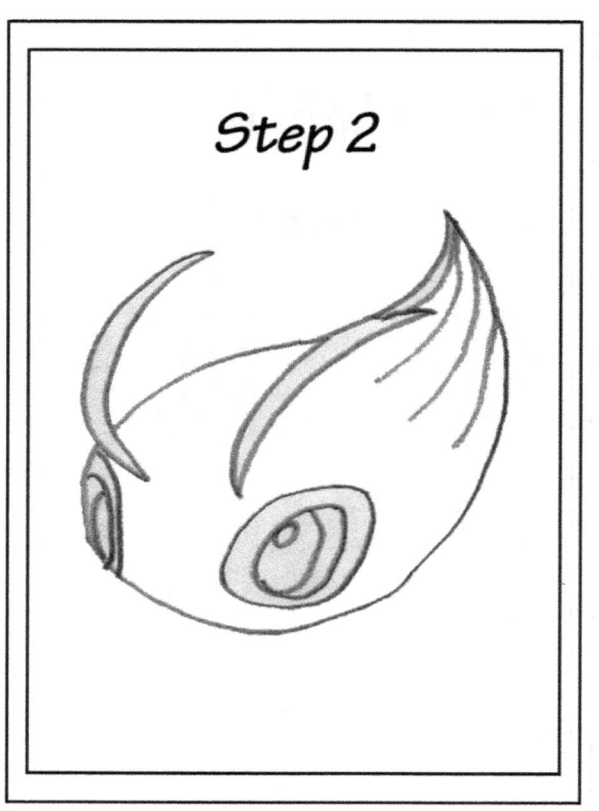

Step 3

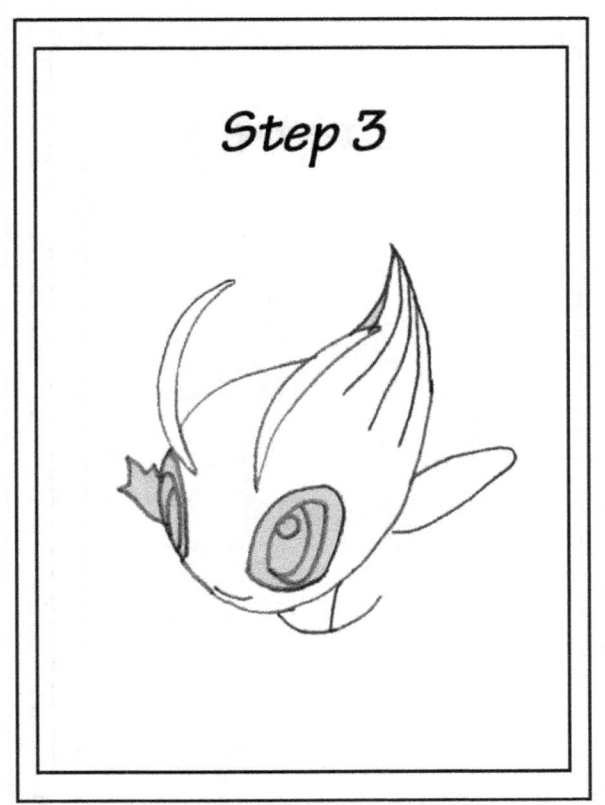

Step 4

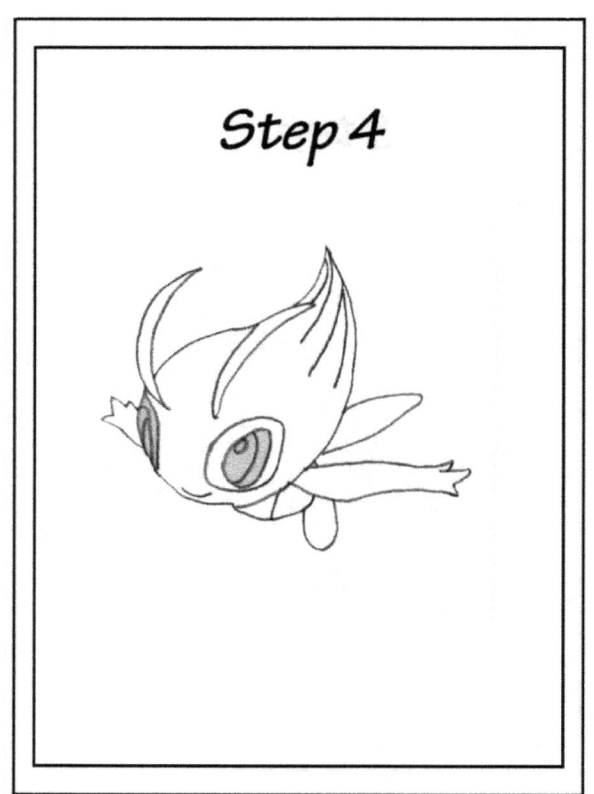

Hypnotize

Step 1

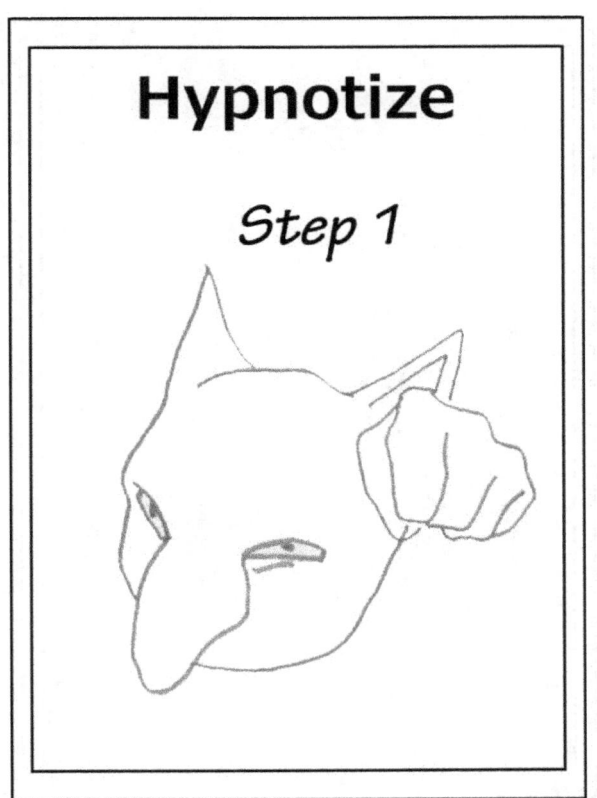

Step 2

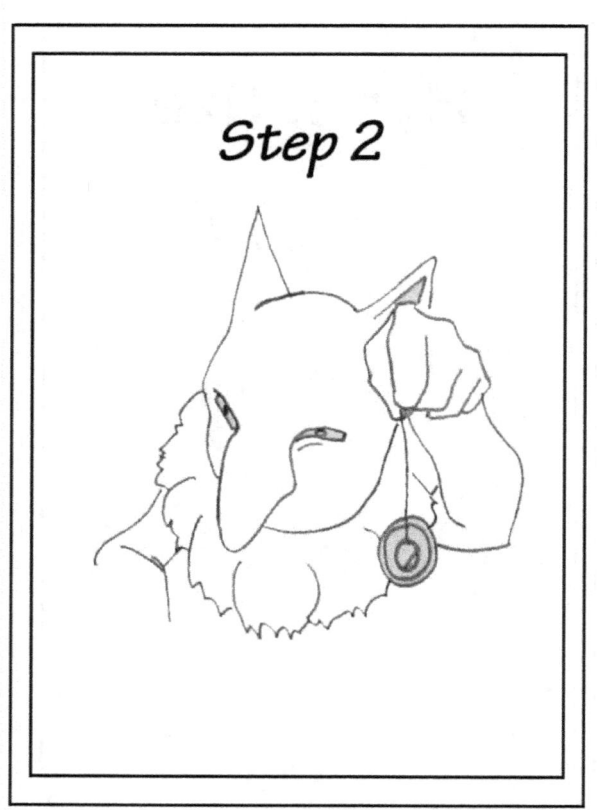

Step 3

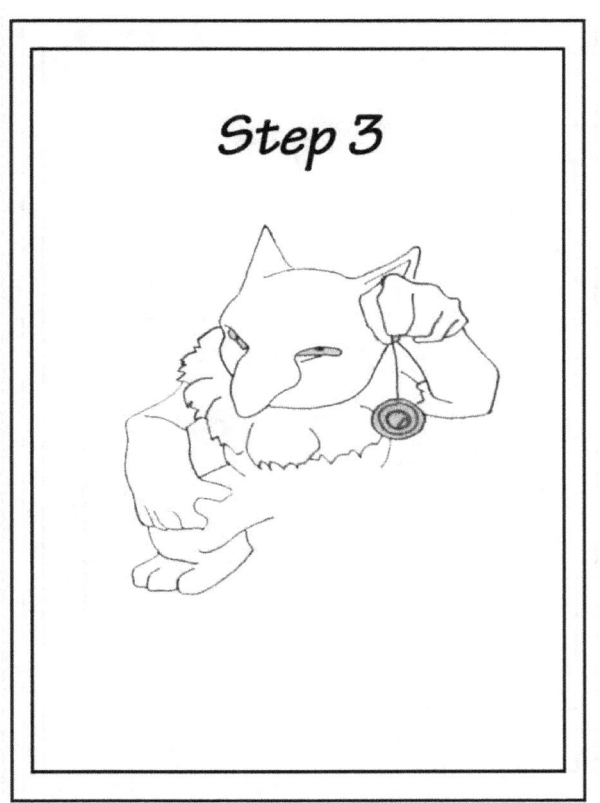

Step 4

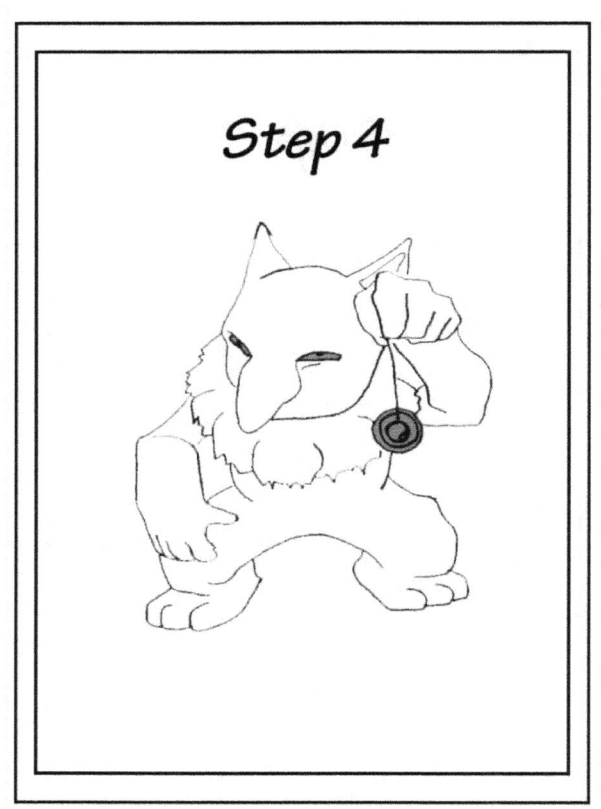

Fletchlins

Step 1

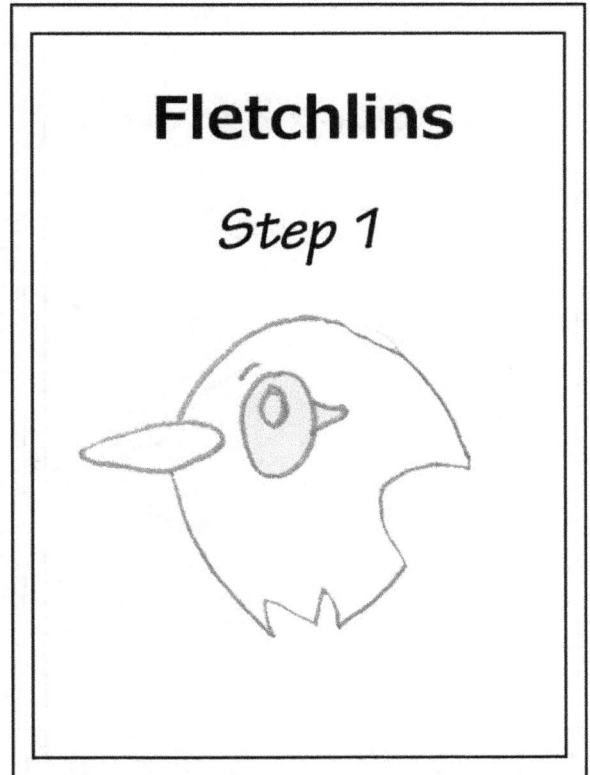

Step 2

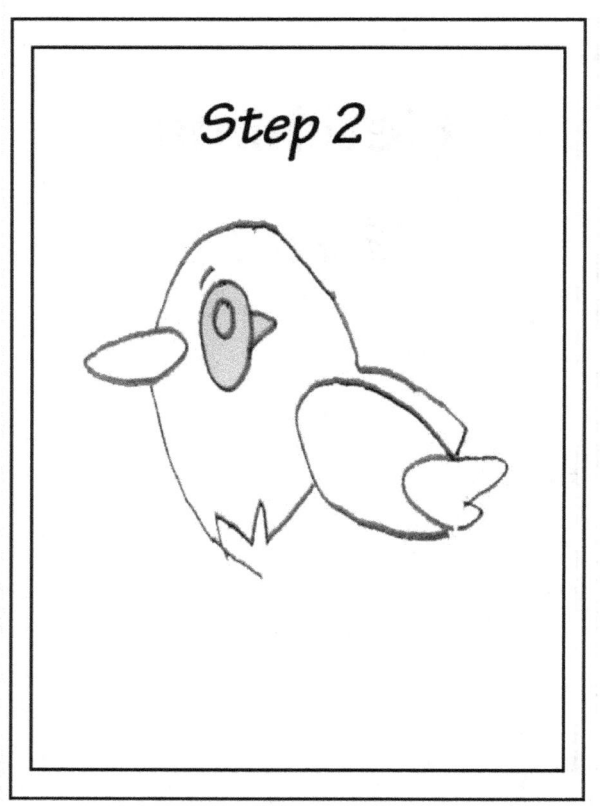

Step 3

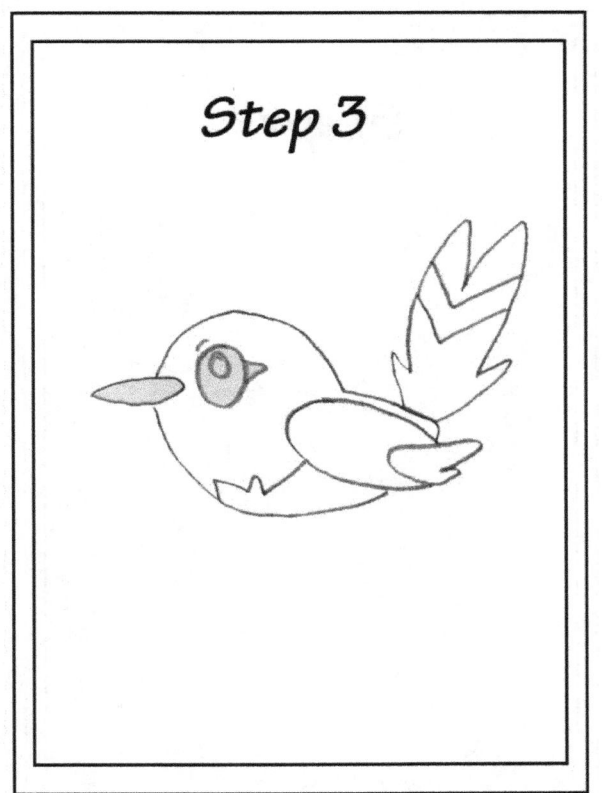

Step 4

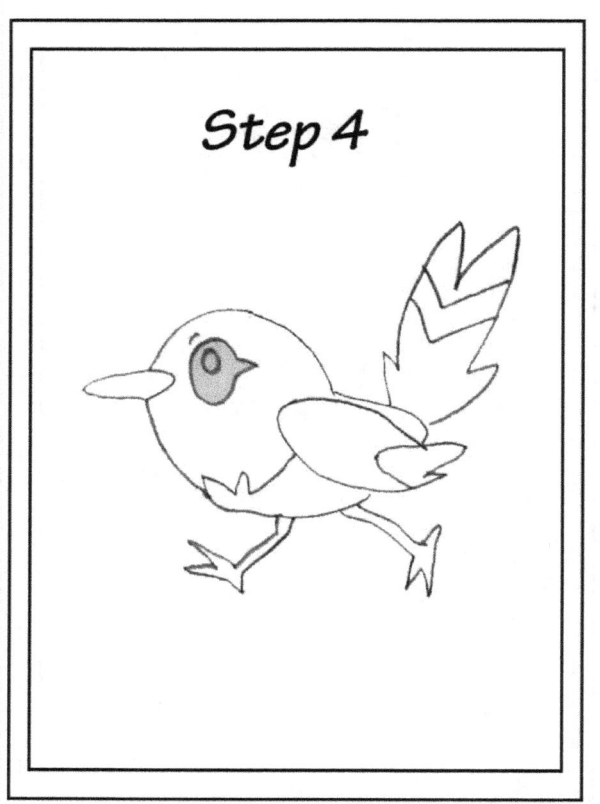

Marshtomp

Step 1

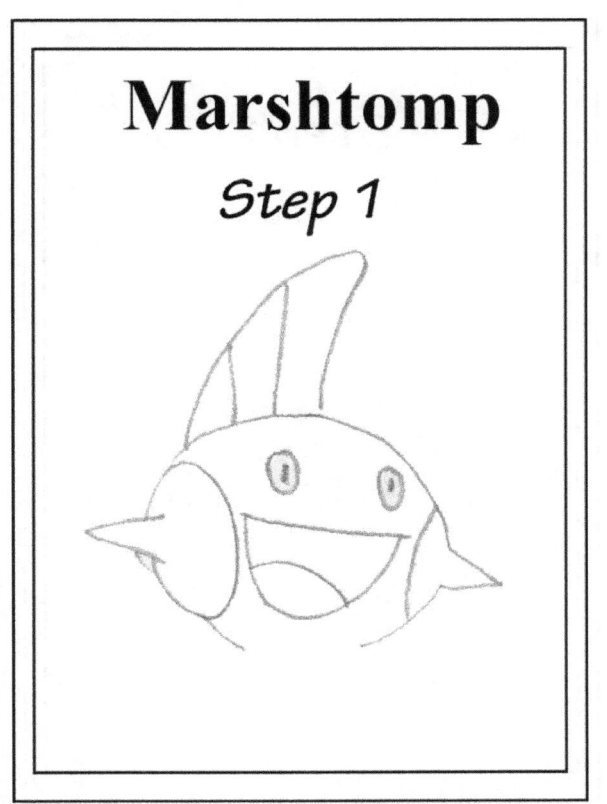

Step 2

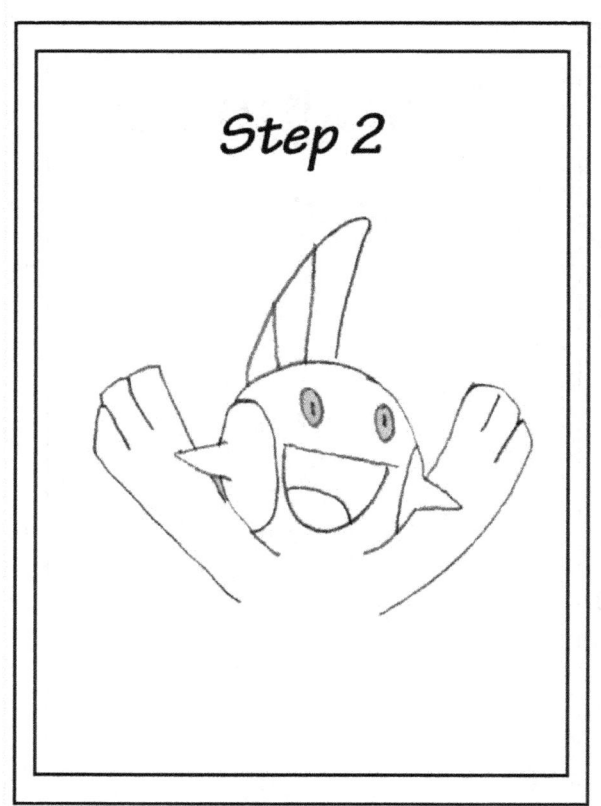

Step 3

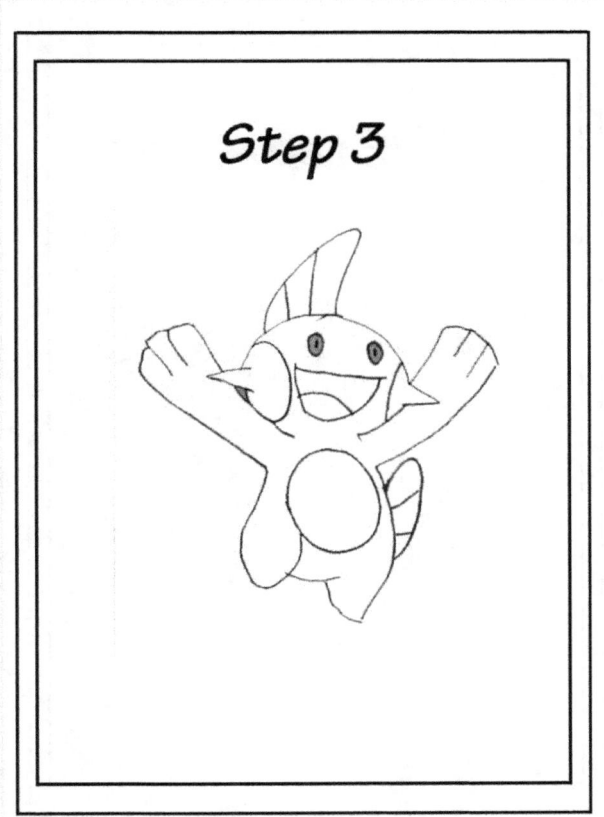

Step 4

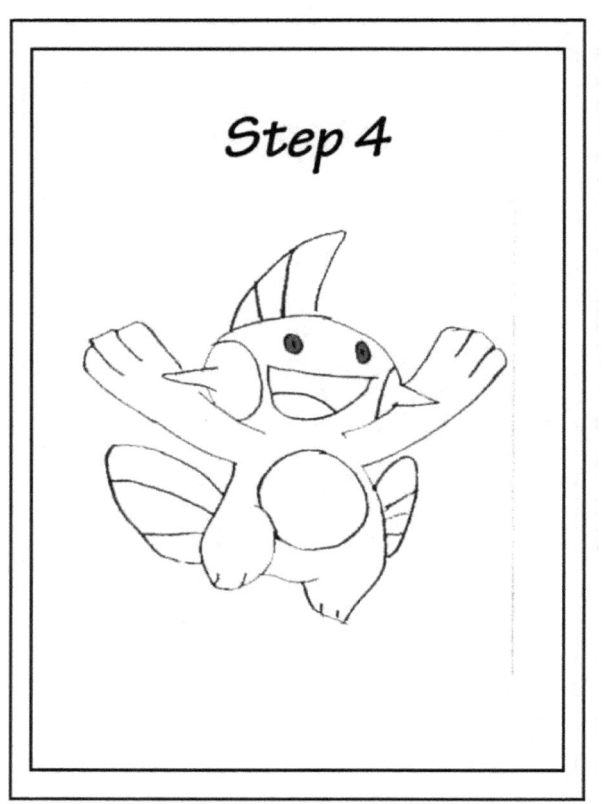

Blaziken

Step 1

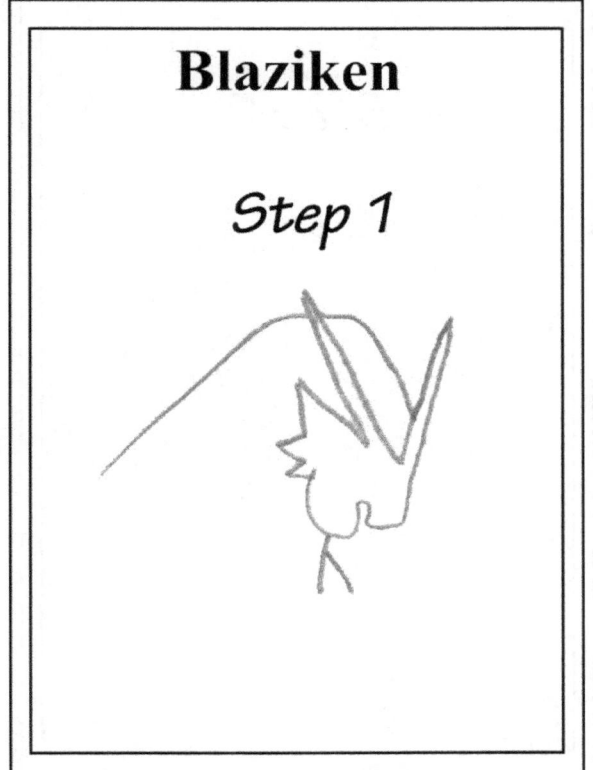

Step 2

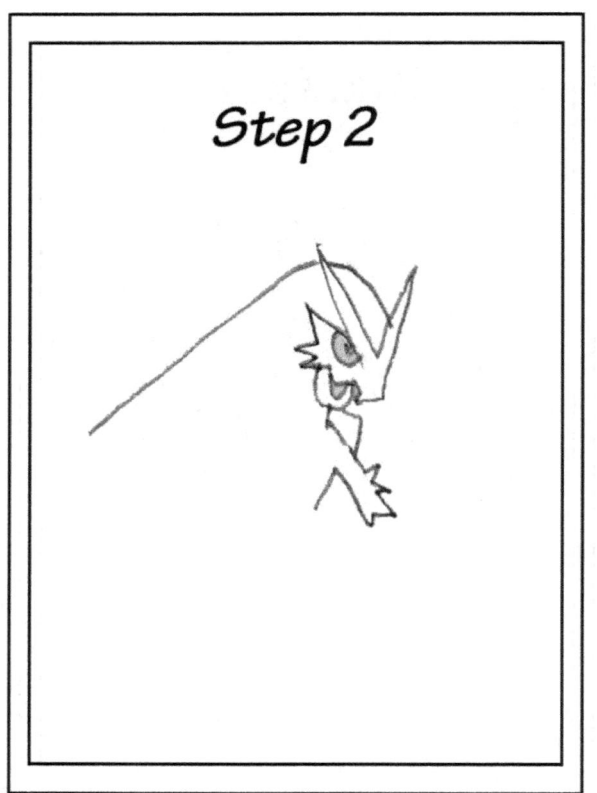

Step 3

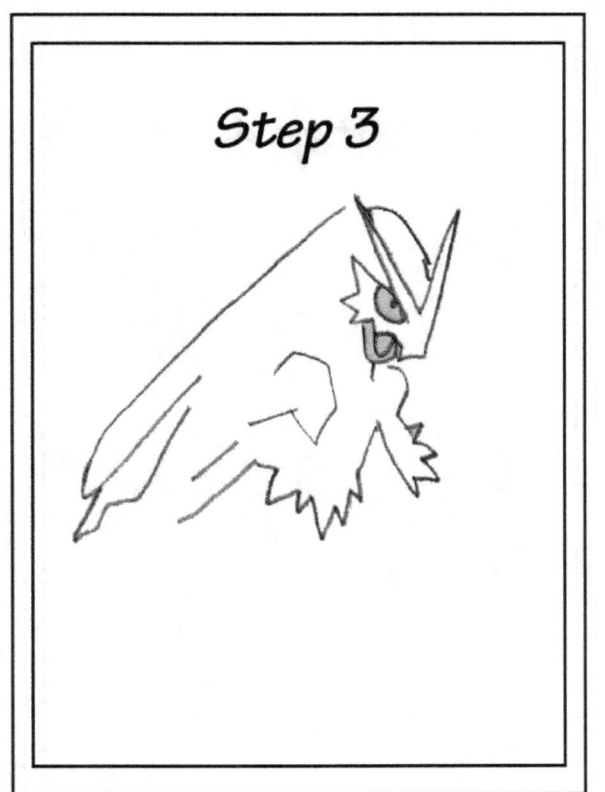

Step 4

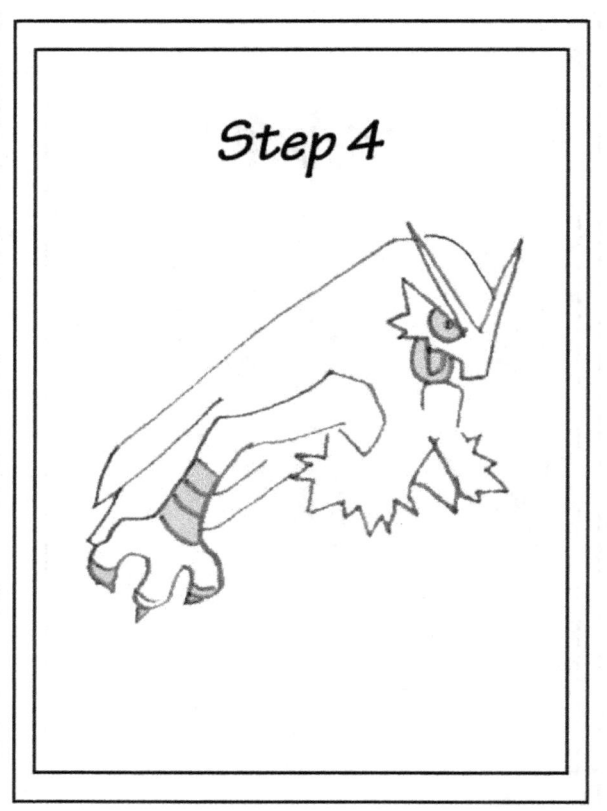

Step 5

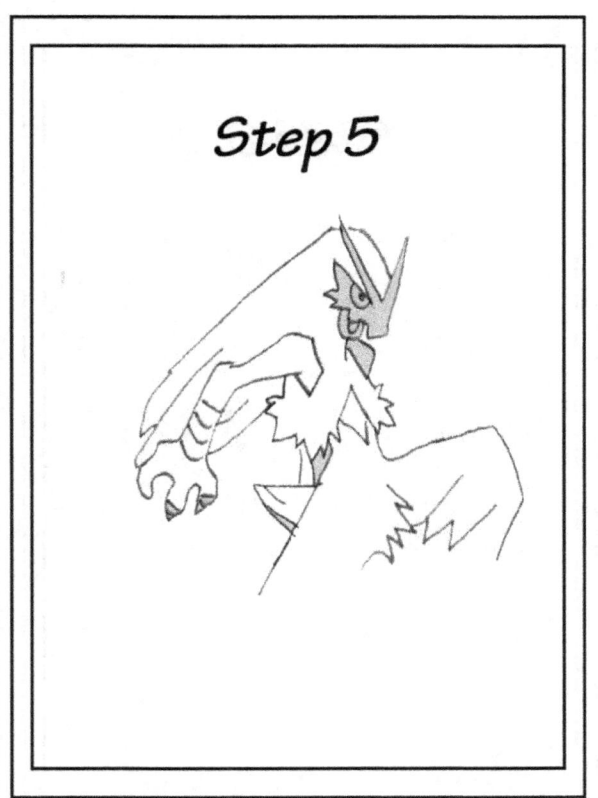

Step 6

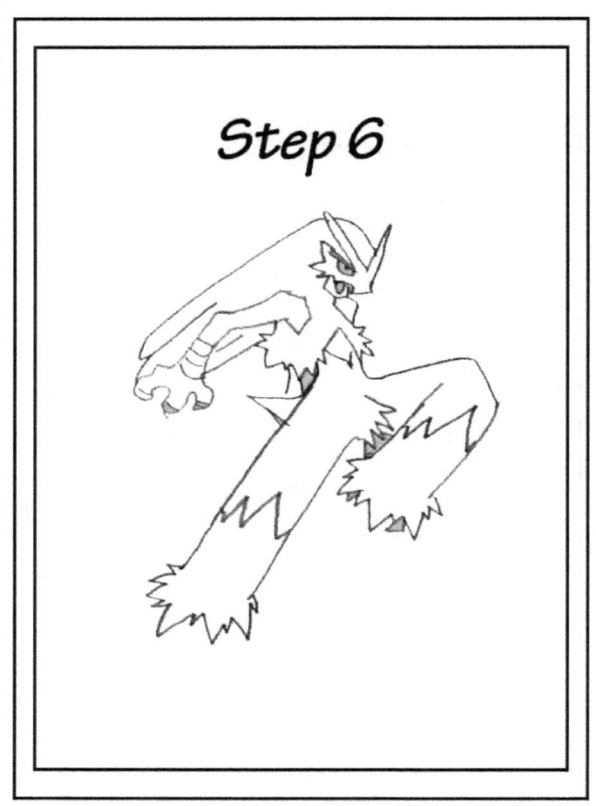

Treecko

Step 1

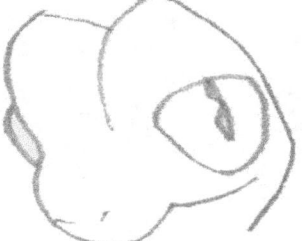

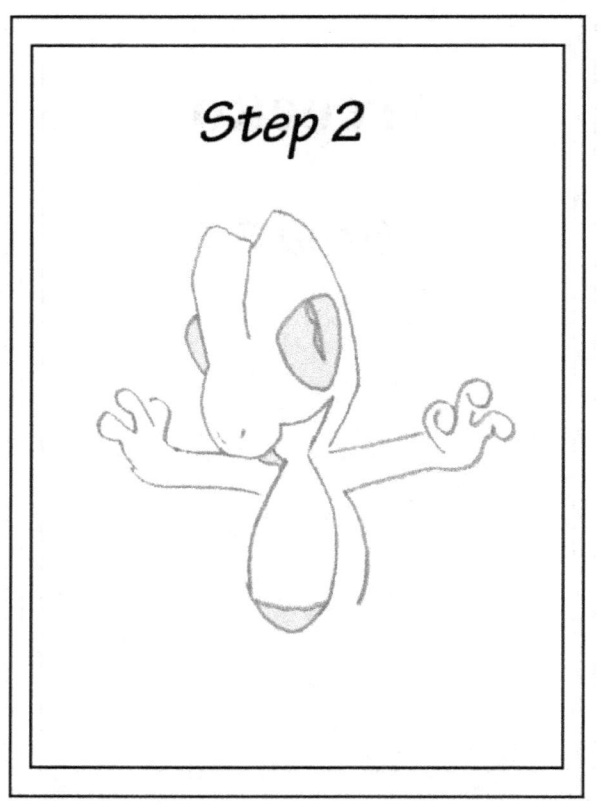

Step 2

Step 3

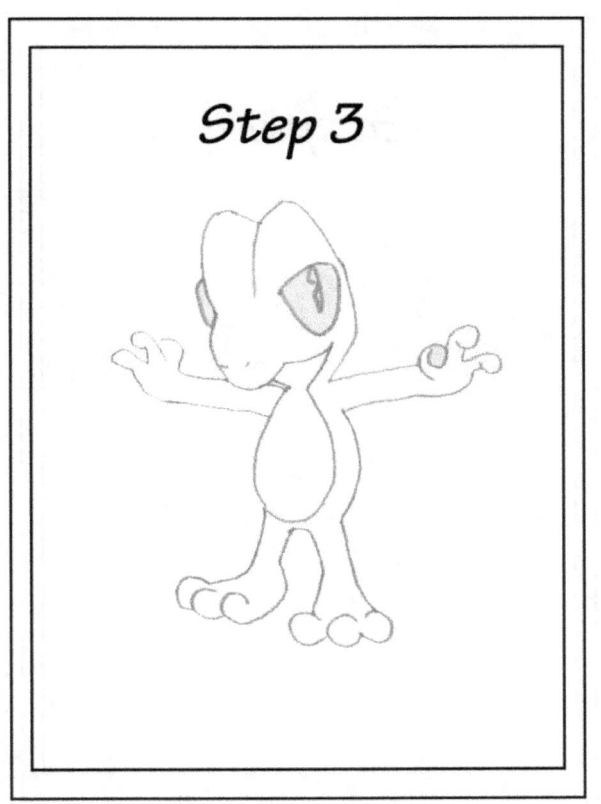

Step 4

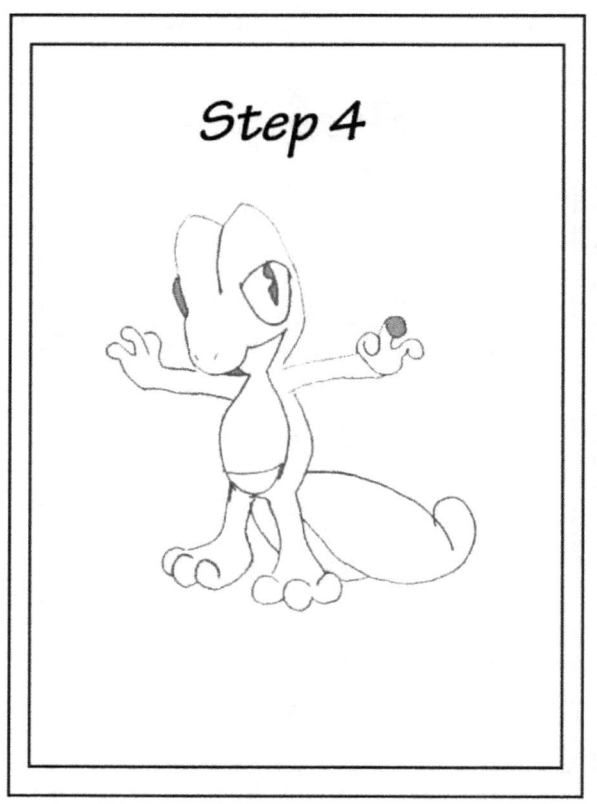